C Programming Success in a Day

BY SAM KEY

Beginners' Guide To Fast, Easy And Efficient Learning Of C Programming

3rd Edition

Table of Contents

Introduction

I want to thank you and congratulate you for purchasing the book, "C Programming Success in a Day – Beginners guide to fast, easy and efficient learning of Cc programming".

C. is one of the most popular and most used programming languages back then and today. Many expert developers have started with learning C in order to become knowledgeable in computer programming. In some grade schools and high schools, C programming is included on their curriculum.

If you are having doubts learning the language, do not. C is actually easy to learn. Compared to C++, C is much simpler and offer little. You do not need spend years to become a master of this language.

This book will tackle the basics when it comes to C. It will cover the basic functions you need in order to create programs that can produce output and accept input. Also, in the later chapters, you will learn how to make your program capable of simple thinking. And lastly, the last chapters will deal with teaching you how to create efficient programs with the help of loops.

Anyway, before you start programming using C, you need to get some things ready. First, you will need a compiler. A compiler is a program that will translate, compile, or convert your lines of code as an executable file. It means that, you will need a compiler for you to be able to run the program you have developed.

In case you are using this book as a supplementary source of information and you are taking a course of C, you might already have a compiler given to you by your instructor. If you are not, you can get one of the compilers that are available on the internet from MinGW.org.

You will also need a text editor. One of the best text editors you can use is Notepad++. It is free and can be downloadable from the internet. Also, it works well with MinGW's compiler.

In case you do not have time to configure or install those programs, you can go and get Microsoft's Visual C++ program. It contains all the things you need in order to practice developing programs using C or C++.

The content of this book was simplified in order for you to comprehend the ideas and practices in developing programs in C easily. Thanks again for purchasing this book. I hope you enjoy it!

Chapter 1: Program Structure and Foundation

When you look at the code used in C language, you will notice that it is highly structured, which makes it a bit easier to understand. It is actually a high level programming language, which means it uses some phrases and words that may be familiar or meaningful to human readers. Dennis Ritchie, the creator developed this programming language, he intended it to be a general purpose language. Eventually, it was used to develop the UNIX operating system. It was first implemented in 1972.

This means that all the Unix applications and the entire operating system itself was built on the foundation of the C programming language. Nowadays, this programming language is used to develop many different applications.

Benefits of Using C Language

The following are some of the benefits that have been cited by experts and other programmers who have used it:

- The code used for C language can be compiled on many different computer systems. It is not restricted to one type of system only.
- It is powerful enough to handle many low level computing activities.
- The programs that have been developed using this language have proven to be quite efficient.
- It is a structured language and you can easily decipher the meaning of the code.
- Many new programmers have found that the C language is really easy to learn.

Of course, there are a lot of other interesting facts about C language. It is the most widely used programming language to create various systems. It is the next step from the B language (1970). The entire language was formalized by ANSI (American National Standard Institute) in 1988.

C was initially designed to create operating systems. You have to understand that that fact alone presents a lot of serious advantages. For one thing, the code created using this language can run nearly as fast as some low level languages such as Assembly Language. However unlike Assembly, C is better structured and easier to learn even for anyone who has no background in programming. C language has been used in the development of utilities, language interpreters, data bases, more modern programs, network drivers, print spoolers, text editors, assemblers, language compilers, and operating systems.

Character Set and Reserved Words

C language uses a particular character set as well as other terms that are exclusive to the operation of the code. Some of these terms are user supplied, which means that the programmer has discretion on what terms to use for certain parts of the code. However, there are key words and reserved terms that cannot be used by a programmer since they provide a special meaning when they are compiled or translated into computer executable code.

The following are the characters that are allowed in C language: all upper case letters from A to Z, all lower case letters from a to z, and all digits from 0 to 9.

Note that there are special characters in C language that may not be freely used by programmers. These special characters have a different meaning in C language. The special characters include the following:

- \
- -
- |
- /
- *
- !
- ^
- "
- }
- {
- &
- '
- [
-]
- %
- :
- $
- ;
-)
- (
- −
- .
- >
- <
- '

Characters Used to Indicate White Space

White space such as form feed, carriage return, tab, new lines, and blank spaces are also part of the language. They may be used with certain specifications.

Keywords

As stated earlier, there are certain terms that are important as to how the code is executed. These certain key words may not be coined by programmers. These are reserved terms and they have been defined by ANSI. They include the following: int, while, auto, volatile, break, void, case, unsigned, char, union, const, typedef, continue, switch, goto, default, struct, do, static, double, sizeof, else, signed, enum, short, extern, return, float, register, for, and long.

Note that these terms do not yet include key words that are used in other versions of C. Instance, Turbo C has these extra reserved terms: cdecl, huge, near, pascal, interrupt, far, and asm.

To give you some sort of idea what these terms mean, a few short definitions will be included below. Note that some of these terms will be discussed at length in other places of this book.

volatile

This is used to define an object in the code that can be modified by computer hardware. The modifications have no specifics.

void

This term is used to indicate that functions in C language will not make use of arguments thus these functions will not return or provide any value.

union

This term indicates that variables of different types are classed or included within a single name.

typedef

This part of the code associates an identifier to a type.

struct

This creates a structure, which can be used to group together different variable types.

static

This declares a storage structure who's value will not change for the entire duration of the program.

register

This defines a variable that is behaves faster compared to regular variables declared in C.

sizeof

This is used to measure the amount of bytes that are stored in a single object.

return

This is used to terminate the operation of functions in C. You will typically see this at the end of a code.

unsigned, signed, long, and short

These are type modifiers. They are used to define and alter fundamental data types.

int

This key word is used to declare a variable that contains integers.

goto

This is a rather common piece of code. You can find it in other programming languages as well (e.g. BASIC). This term makes the execution of the program to jump to a specific set of instructions or a different function or routine.

for

This is a reserved term that is used for program looping.

extern

This indicates or declares a variable that is outside of the current function. The variable that it creates can be modified by other functions in the code.

enum

This creates a type of integer data whose value is a constant.

if - else

This creates a conditional within the execution of a program. It allows the program to execute different commands depending on certain conditions.

float, double

These terms declare variables that are floating type numbers. The term float creates a single precision variable while double creates a double precision variable.

do - while

This also creates a loop in the program execution. However, it also includes a conditional statement. This means that a set of instructions or code will be executed while a certain condition remains true.

const

This makes the value of a variable or even the value of a pointer (will be discussed in detail later) to be unchangeable for the duration of the execution of the program.

char

This keyword is used to create a variable that will contain a character value.

default, case, switch

These statements are used to test the value of different expressions in the code.

continue – break

The term "break" is used to go out of a loop inside a code. The term "continue" is used to skip certain instructions inside a loop.

auto

This code indicates that a certain variable is local to a certain function within the code. Outside of that function and in other sections of the code, that variable will be meaningless.

Identifiers in C Language

When you write code in C, you will usually create data structures that contain different values. For instance, when you use int within a code, you are actually creating a variable (i.e. a data structure that changes value – just like in algebra) that will contain only integers. Here's an example:

int xy;
int ab;

In these two examples, the code is creating two variables – xy and ab. Both of these variables will contain whole numbers (i.e. integers). The terms xy and ab are called identifiers. Of course, programmers who write codes using C just can't create any identifier. There are rules for creating these identifiers. They are the following:

1. You can use either upper case letters or lower case letters when making these identifiers. You can also use numbers to go with those letters. You can also add an underscore.
2. The first letter of an identifier must be either an underscore or a letter. In actual practice, almost all programmers avoid starting their identifier names with underscores since it can interfere with other processes when compiled especially when it comes to other system names.
3. Note that even though any identifier name can be any length, in principle, in actual fact compilers will only use up to 31 characters when processing identifier names.
4. You cannot use any of the reserved words and character sets in C language. The only special character you can use is an underscore.

Chapter 2: The Data Types in C Language

One of the many things that you will do when you code in C is to manipulate and make use of data. There are several types of data that can be used in this programming language. A data type can be a certain value or even a set of values. The programs you write will be more useful when they can make use, store, and organize data so that they will become useful to end users.

Uses of Different Data Types

Data types in this programming language can be used to identify different variables when they are declared. Variables will be discussed in detail later. Functions will be discussed later on and these functions will also return different data types that will be used in various parts of a program. Functions will also be discussed much later.

Primary and Secondary Data Types

There are primary and secondary data types in C. The primary data types are the following:

- Void
- Character
- Float
- Integer
- Double

The secondary types of data in this programming language are as follows:

- Union

- Structure
- Pointer
- Array

Note that there are also built-in data structures in C. They include both the primary and secondary data types mentioned above. They are called built-in simply because these data structures are already part and parcel of the C language library. The fundamental data types include pointer, float, double, char, int, and void. From these fundamental data types are formed the derived data types which include structure, string, and array.

However, this programming language is also dynamic. Programmers can also define their own data structures. But that is more of an advanced topic, which you should learn after you have mastered the basics mentioned here in this book.

The Fundamental Data Types

The following are short descriptions of the fundamental data types. They will be discussed in greater detail in the other parts of this book. The definitions here will help you grasp the different notions used in C.

char *, float *, int*	These data types are used to identify a data type called pointers (will be discussed in detail later)
double, float	These are used to denote floating point data
char	This is used to designate a single character
int	This is used to denote or declare integers (numeric data)
void	This is data type that is used to denote no value

The following are called derived data types. You can say that a sequence of certain fundamental data types can be used to create derived data types. Consider the following definitions.

structure	This data type is a collection of variables that are related to one another. The variables may be of the same fundamental data type or it may consist of different fundamental data types.
string	This data type is a sequence of different char data types. When you combine different characters and arrange them into a sequence then you have a character string.
array	This data type can be arranged as a sequence or an entire table. It can contain different types of variables of the same fundamental data type.

You will learn other data types as you move on to other chapters of this book.

Variables vs. Constants

Variables will be discussed at length in a later portion of this book. However, we'll touch on them lightly here to help you distinguish the differences between variables and constants and how they are used in C language.

Simply put, variables refer to a storage location in your computer's memory. Its primary purpose is to hold data temporarily. Each variable in C should be given a unique name. The name you give each variable is only a symbolic name and is only meaningful to humans while reading the code. Your compiler will assign a machine readable name to the actual variable or memory address being used.

Since variable names are identifiers, then you should stick to the rules on creating identifier names, which was already mentioned elsewhere in this book. As a quick review here are the rules in simple terms:

Only alphanumeric characters are allowed (upper case and lower case) and underscores. Maximum length is 31 characters. Names must begin with a letter.

The Different C Language Constants

Constants on the other hand are also like variables. However, unlike variables, the value contained in constants can't be changed. There are different constants used in C language, which include the following:

- Integer constants
- Floating point constants
- Character constants
- Escape constants
- String constants
- Enumeration constants

Enumeration Constants: the enum constant is used in any declaration of enumeration types. For example:

enum color {blue, red, yellow, green};

String Constants: you will see these constants in the code as any text that is enclosed within double quotation marks. Here are several examples on how to use string constants:

Regular string constant – "okay"
Null string constant – ""
String constant with white spaces – "   "
String constant with one character – "a"
String printed on a new line – "this goes to the next line"

Escape Sequences: escape sequences are used to display quotation marks, tabs, and hard returns. A backslash is used as a break from the usual way a compiler will interpret certain lines of code. Here are some examples of escape sequences:

Null character – \o
Question mark – \?
Double quotes – \"
Single quote – \'
Backslash – \\
Vertical tab – \v
Horizontal tab – \t
Return – \r
Newline – \n
Form feed – \f
Backspace – \b

Character Constants: character constants appear as single characters that are enclosed in single quotes. For example: 'o'

Floating Point Constants: floating point constants refer to numbers with a fractional component. It also refers to numeric values with exponents. Here are a few examples:

-0.11E-4
0.00143
-1.0

Integer Constants: integer constants are constants that are associated with a number. These numbers should not have any fractional parts. They should also not have an exponent. There are three different types of integer constants in C. They are decimal, octal, and hexadecimal constants.

Examples of decimal constants include 22, -9, and 0. Examples of octal constants include 033, 077, and 021. Examples of hexadecimal constants include 0x521 and 0x7f.

Note that hexadecimal constants usually start with a "0x." You can also use lower case letters for hexadecimal constants. As you observe from the examples above, octal constants usually start with 0.

Chapter 3: Hello World – the Basics

When coding a C program, you must start your code with the function 'main'. By the way, a function is a collection of action that aims to achieve one or more goals. For example, a vegetable peeler has one function, which is to remove a skin of a vegetable. The peeler is composed of parts (such as the blade and handle) that will aid you to perform its function. A C function is also composed of such components and they are the lines of codes within it.

Also, take note that in order to make your coding life easier, you will need to include some prebuilt headers or functions from your compiler.

To give you an idea on what C code looks like, check the sample below:

```
#include <stdio.h>
int main()
{
    printf( "Hello World!\n" );
    getchar();
    return 0;
}
```

As you can see in the first line, the code used the #include directive to include the stdio.h in the program. In this case, the stdio.h will provide you with access to functions such as printf and getchar.

Main Declaration

After that, the second line contains int main(). This line tells the compiler that there exist a function named main. The int in the line indicates that the function main will return an integer or number.

Curly Braces

The next line contains a curly brace. In C programming, curly braces indicate the start and end of a code block or a function. A code block is a series of codes joined together in a series. When a function is called by the program, all the line of codes inside it will be executed.

Printf()

The printf function, which follows the opening curly brace is the first line of code in your main function or code block. Like the function main, the printf also have a code block within it, which is already created and included since you included <stdio.h> in your program. The function of printf is to print text into your program's display window.

Beside printf is the value or text that you want to print. It should be enclosed in parentheses to abide standard practice. The value that the code want to print is Hello World!. To make sure that printf to recognize that you want to print a string and display the text properly, it should be enclosed inside double quotation marks.

By the way, in programming, a single character is called a character while a sequence of characters is called a string.

Escape Sequence

You might have noticed that the sentence is followed by a \n. In C, \n means new line. Since your program will have problems if you put a new line or press enter on the value of the printf, it is best to use its text equivalent or the escape sequence of the new line.

By the way, the most common escape sequences used in C are:

\t = tab

\f = new page

\r = carriage return

\b = backspace

\v = vertical tab

Semicolons

After the last parenthesis, a semicolon follows. And if you look closer, almost every line of code ends with it. The reasoning behind that is that the semicolon acts as an indicator that it is the end of the line of code or command. Without it, the compiler will think that the following lines are included in the printf function. And if that happens, you will get a syntax error.

Getchar()

Next is the getchar() function. Its purpose is to receive user input from the keyboard. Many programmers use it as a method on pausing a program and letting the program wait for the user to interact with it before it executes the next line of code. To make the program move through after the getchar() function, the user must press the enter key.

In the example, if you compile or run it without getchar(), the program will open the display or the console, display the text, and then immediately close. Without the break provided by the getchar() function, the computer will execute those commands instantaneously. And the program will open and close so fast that you will not be able to even see the Hello World text in the display.

Return Statement

The last line of code in the function is return 0. The return statement is essential in function blocks. When the program reaches this part, the return statement will tell the program its value. Returning the 0 value will make the program interpret that the function or code block that was executed successfully.

And at the last line of the example is the closing curly brace. It signifies that the program has reached the end of the function.

It was not that not hard, was it? With that example alone, you can create simple programs that can display text. Play around with it a bit and familiarize yourself with C's basic syntax.

Chapter 4: Basic Input Output

After experimenting with what you learned in the previous chapter, you might have realized that it was not enough. It was boring. And just displaying what you typed in your program is a bit useless.

This time, this chapter will teach you how to create a program that can interact with the user. Check this code example:

```c
#include <stdio.h>
int main()
{
    int number_container;
    printf( "Enter any number you want! " );
    scanf( "%d", &number_container );
    printf( "The number you entered is %d", number_container );
    getchar();
    return 0;
}
```

Variables

You might have noticed the int number_container part in the first line of the code block. int number_container is an example of variable declaration. To declare a variable in C, you must indicate the variable type first, and then the name of the variable name.

In the example, int was indicated as the variable or data type, which means the variable is an integer. There are other variable types in C such as float for floating-point numbers, char for characters, etc. Alternatively, the name number_container was indicated as the variable's name or identifier.

Variables are used to hold values throughout the program and code blocks. The programmer can let them assign a value to it and retrieve its value when it is needed.

For example:

int number_container;

number_container = 3;

printf ("The variables value is %d", number_container);

In that example, the first line declared that the program should create an integer variable named number_container. The second line assigned a value to the variable. And the third line makes the program print the text together with the value of the variable. When executed, the program will display:

The variables value is 3

You might have noticed the %d on the printf line on the example. The %d part indicates that the next value that will be printed will be an integer. Also, the quotation on the printf ended after %d. Why is that?

In order to print the value of a variable, it must be indicated with the double quotes. If you place double quotes on the variables name, the compiler will treat it as a literal string. If you do this:

int number_container;

number_container = 3;

printf ("The variables value is number_container");

The program will display:

The variables value is number_container

By the way, you can also use %i as a replacement for %d.

Assigning a value to a variable is simple. Just like in the previous example, just indicate the name of variable, follow it with an equal sign, and declare its value.

When creating variables, you must make sure that each variable will have unique names. Also, the variables should never have the same name as functions. In addition, you can declare multiple variables in one line by using commas. Below is an example:

int first_variable, second_variable, third_variable;

Those three variables will be int type variables. And again, never forget to place a semicolon after your declaration.

When assigning a value or retrieving the value of a variable, make sure that you declare its existence first. If not, the compiler will return an error since it will try to access something that does not exist yet.

Scanf()

In the first example in this chapter, you might have noticed the scanf function. The scanf function is also included in the <stdio.h>. Its purpose is to retrieve text user input from the user.

After the program displays the 'Enter any number you want' text, it will proceed in retrieving a number from the user. The cursor will be appear after the text since the new line escape character was no included in the printf.

The cursor will just blink and wait for the user to enter any characters or numbers. To let the program get the number the user typed and let it proceed to the next line of code, he must press the Enter key. Once he does that, the program will display the text 'The number you entered is' and the value of the number the user inputted a while ago.

To make the scanf function work, you must indicate the data type it needs to receive and the location of the variable where the value that scanf will get will be stored. In the example:

scanf("%d", &number_container);

The first part "%d" indicates that the scanf function must retrieve an integer. On the other hand, the next part indicates the location of the variable. You must have noticed the ampersand placed in front of the variable's name. The ampersand retrieves the location of the variable and tells it to the function.

Unlike the typical variable value assignment, scanf needs the location of the variable instead of its name alone. Due to that, without the ampersand, the function will not work.

Math or Arithmetic Operators

Aside from simply giving number variables with values by typing a number, you can assign values by using math operators. In C, you can add, subtract, multiply, and divide numbers and assign the result to variables directly. For example:

int sum;

sum = 1 + 2;

If you print the value of sum, it will return a 3, which is the result of the addition of 1 and 2. By the way, the + sign is for addition, - for subtraction, * for multiplication, and / for division.

With the things you have learned as of now, you can create a simple calculator program. Below is an example code:

```
#include <stdio.h>
int main()
{
        int first_addend, second_addend, sum;
```

```
printf( "Enter the first addend! " );
scanf( "%d", &first_addend );
printf( "\nEnter the second addend! " );
scanf( "%d", &second_addend );
sum = first_addend + second_addend;
printf( "The sum of the two numbers is %d", sum );
getchar();
return 0;
}
```

Chapter 5: Conditional Statements

The calculator program seems nice, is it not? However, the previous example limits you on creating programs that only uses one operation, which is a bit disappointing. Well, in this chapter, you can improve that program with the help of if or conditional statements. And of course, learning this will improve your overall programming skills. This is the part where you will be able to make your program 'think'.

'If' statements can allow you to create branches in your code blocks. Using them allows you to let the program think and perform specific functions or actions depending on certain variables and situations. Below is an example:

```
#include <stdio.h>
int main()
{
    int some_number;
    printf( "Welcome to Guess the Magic Number program. \n" );
    printf( "Guess the magic number to win. \n" );
    printf( "Type the magic number and press Enter: " );
    scanf( "%d", &some_number );
    if ( some_number == 3 ) {
        printf( "You guessed the right number! " );
    }
```

```
    getchar();

    return 0;

}
```

In the example, the if statement checked if the value of the variable some_number is equal to number 3. In case the user entered the number 3 on the program, the comparison between the variable some_number and three will return TRUE since the value of some_number 3 is true. Since the value that the if statement received was TRUE, then it will process the code block below it. And the result will be:

You guessed the right number!

If the user input a number other than three, the comparison will return a FALSE value. If that happens, the program will skip the code block in the if statement and proceed to the next line of code after the if statement's code block.

By the way, remember that you need to use the curly braces to enclosed the functions that you want to happen in case your if statement returns TRUE. Also, when inserting if statement, you do not need to place a semicolon after the if statement or its code block's closing curly brace. However, you will still need to place semicolons on the functions inside the code blocks of your if statements.

TRUE and FALSE

The if statement will always return TRUE if the condition is satisfied. For example, the condition in the if statement is 10 > 2. Since 10 is greater than 2, then it is true. On the other hand, the if statement will always return FALSE if the condition is not satisfied. For example, the condition in the if statement is 5 < 5. Since 5 is not less than 5, then the statement will return a FALSE.

Note that if statements only return two results: TRUE and FALSE. In computer programming, the number equivalent to TRUE is any nonzero number. In some cases, it is only the number 1. On the other hand, the number equivalent of FALSE is zero.

Operators

Also, if statements use comparison, Boolean, or relational and logical operators. Some of those operators are:

== – equal to

!= – not equal to

> – greater than

< – less than

>= – greater than or equal to

<= – less than or equal to

Quick Tips – Other Operators in C Language

This programming language makes use of several operators to define the value of different variables. You have already encountered some of these operators earlier. The C language operators include arithmetic operators, assignment operators, increment operators, decrement operators, relational operators, conditional operators, logical operators, bitwise operators, and bitwise operators.

Arithmetic operators include the following:

Division: "/"
Multiplication: "*"
Subtraction: "-" (can also be used as unary minus)
Addition: "+" (can also be used as unary plus)

Increment vs. Decrement Operators

"++" is the operator for increment while "−" is the operator for decrements. They make one unit increments or decrements to the value of an object. Note that increment and decrement operators can be placed before or after a variable. When these operators prefix a variable they will increment the value of the variable first and then return the new value. However, if they postfix a variable then the value of the variable will be returned first and then only will this operator increment or decrement the original value.

Assignment Operators

The equal sign is the assignment operator in C language. It assigns a value to the variable. Note that the variable should be on the left side of the operator and the value should be on the right. For example: "a = 25"

Logical Operators

These operators combine expressions. There are three logical operators used in C. They are "&&" (logical and), "||" (logical or), and "!" (logical not).

Bitwise Operators

C language also involves bit level programming. It will not be covered in this book but at least you know what operators are involved or used. The bitwise operators in C language are the following:

> Shift right: >>
> Shift left: <<
> Bitwise complement: ~
> Bitwise exclusive OR: ^
> Bitwise OR: |
> Bitwise AND: &

Else Statement

There will be times that you would want your program to do something else in case your if statement return FALSE. And that is what the else statement is for. Check the example below:

```
#include <stdio.h>

int main()

{

    int some_number;

    printf( "Welcome to Guess the Magic Number program. \n" );

    printf( "Guess the magic number to win. \n" );

    printf( "Type the magic number and press Enter: " );

    scanf( "%d", &some_number );

    if ( some_number == 3 ) {

        printf( "You guessed the right number! " );
```

```
    }
    else {
        printf( "Sorry. That is the wrong number" );
    }
    getchar();
    return 0;
}
```

If ever the if statement returns FALSE, the program will skip next to the else statement immediately. And since the if statement returns FALSE, it will immediately process the code block inside the else statement.

For example, if the number the user inputted on the program is 2, the if statement will return a FALSE. Due to that, the else statement will be processed, and the program will display:

Sorry. That is the wrong number

On the other hand, if the if statement returns TRUE, it will process the if statement's code block, but it will bypass all the succeeding else statements below it.

Else If

If you want more conditional checks on your program, you will need to take advantage of else if. Else if is a combination of the if and else statement. It will act like an else statement, but instead of letting the program execute the code block below it, it will perform another check as if it was an if statement. Below is an example:

```c
#include <stdio.h>
int main()
{
    int some_number;
    printf( "Welcome to Guess the Magic Number program. \n" );
    printf( "Guess the magic number to win. \n" );
    printf( "Type the magic number and press Enter: " );
    scanf( "%d", &some_number );
    if ( some_number == 3 ) {
        printf( "You guessed the right number! " );
    }
    else if ( some_number > 3 ){
        printf( "Your guess is too high!" );
    }
    else {
        printf( "Your guess is too low!" );
    }
    getchar();
    return 0;
```

}

In case the if statement returns FALSE, the program will evaluate the else if statement. If it returns TRUE, it will execute its code block and ignore the following else statements. However, if it is FALSE, it will proceed on the last else statement, and execute its code block. And just like before, if the first if statement returns true, it will disregard the following else and else if statements.

In the example, if the user inputs 3, he will get the You guessed the right number message. If the user inputs 4 or higher, he will get the Your guess is too high message. And if he inputs any other number, he will get a Your guess is too low message since any number aside from 3 and 4 or higher is automatically lower than 3.

With the knowledge you have now, you can upgrade the example calculator program to handle different operations. Look at the example and study it:

```
#include <stdio.h>
int main()
{
        int first_number, second_number, result, operation;
        printf( "Enter the first number: " );
        scanf( "%d", &first_number );
        printf( "\nEnter the second number: " );
```

```
scanf( "%d", &second_number );
printf ( "What operation would you like to use? \n" );
printf ( "Enter 1 for addition. \n" );
printf ( "Enter 2 for subtraction. \n" );
printf ( "Enter 3 for multiplication. \n" );
printf ( "Enter 4 for division. \n" );
scanf( "%d", &operation );
if ( operation == 1 ) {
        result = first_number + second_number;
        printf( "The sum is %d", result );
}
else if ( operation == 2 ){
        result = first_number - second_number;
        printf( "The difference is %d", result );
}
else if ( operation == 3 ){
        result = first_number * second_number;
        printf( "The product is %d", result );
}
else if ( operation == 4 ){
        result = first_number / second_number;
        printf( "The quotient is %d", result );
}
```

```
else {
        printf( "You have entered an invalid choice." );
}
getchar();
return 0;
}
```

Chapter 6: Looping in C

The calculator's code is getting better, right? As of now, it is possible that you are thinking about the programs that you could create with the usage of the conditional statements.

However, as you might have noticed in the calculator program, it seems kind of painstaking to use. You get to only choose one operation every time you run the program. When the calculation ends, the program closes. And that can be very annoying and unproductive.

To solve that, you must create loops in the program. Loops are designed to let the program execute some of the functions inside its code blocks. It effectively eliminates the need to write some same line of codes. It saves the time of the programmer and it makes the program run more efficiently.

There are four different ways in creating a loop in C. In this chapter, two of the only used and simplest loop method will be discussed. To grasp the concept of looping faster, check the example below:

```c
#include <stdio.h>
int main()
{
        int some_number;
        int guess_result;
        guess_result = 0;
```

```c
printf( "Welcome to Guess the Magic Number program. \n" );
printf( "Guess the magic number to win. \n" );
printf( "You have unlimited chances to guess the number. \n" );

while ( guess_result == 0 ) {

        printf( "Guess the magic number: " );
        scanf( "%d", &some_number );
        if ( some_number == 3 ) {
                printf( "You guessed the right number! \n" );
                guess_result = 1;
        }
        else if ( some_number > 3 ){
                printf( "Your guess is too high! \n" );
                guess_result = 0;
        }
        else {
                printf( "Your guess is too low! \n" );
                guess_result = 0;
        }

}
```

```
    printf( "Thank you for playing. Press Enter to exit this
program." );

    getchar();

    return 0;

}
```

While Loop

In this example, the while loop function was used. The while loop allows the program to execute the code block inside it as long as the condition is met or the argument in it returns TRUE. It is one of the simplest loop function in C. In the example, the condition that the while loop requires is that the guess_result variable should be equal to 0.

As you can see, in order to make sure that the while loop will start, the value of the guess_result variable was set to 0.

If you have not noticed it yet, you can actually nest code blocks within code blocks. In this case, the code block of the if and else statements were inside the code block of the while statement.

Anyway, every time the code reaches the end of the while statement and the guess_result variable is set to 0, it will repeat itself. And to make sure that the program or user experience getting stuck into an infinite loop, a safety measure was included.

In the example, the only way to escape the loop is to guess the magic number. If the if statement within the while code block was satisfied, its code block will run. In that code block, a line of code sets the variable guess_result's value to 1. This effectively prevent the while loop from running once more since the guess_result's value is not 0 anymore, which makes the statement return a FALSE.

Once that happens, the code block of the while loop and the code blocks inside it will be ignored. It will skip to the last printf line, which will display the end program message 'Thank you for playing. Press Enter to exit this program'.

For Loop

The for loop is one of the most handy looping function in C. And its main use is to perform repetitive commands on a set number of times. Below is an example of its use:

```c
#include <stdio.h>
int main()
{
    int some_number;
    int x;
    int y;

    printf( "Welcome to Guess the Magic Number program. \n" );
    printf( "Guess the magic number to win. \n" );
    printf( "You have only three chance of guessing. \n" );
    printf( "If you do not get the correct answer after guessing three times. \n" );
    printf( "This program will be terminated. \n" );
```

```c
for (x = 0; x < 3; x++) {
        y = 3 - x;
        printf( "The number of guesses that you have left is:
%d", y );
        printf( "\nGuess the magic number: " );
        scanf( "%d", &some_number );
        if ( some_number == 3 ) {
                printf( "You guessed the right number! \n" );
                x = 4;
        }
        else if ( some_number > 3 ){
                printf( "Your guess is too high! \n " );
        }
        else {
                printf( "Your guess is too low! \n " );
        }
}
printf( "Press the Enter button to close this program. \n" );
getchar();
getchar();
return 0;
}
```

The for statement's argument section or part requires three things. First, the initial value of the variable that will be used. In this case, the example declared that x = 0. Second, the condition. In the example, the for loop will run until x has a value lower than 3. Third, the variable update line. Every time the for loop loops, the variable update will be executed. In this case, the variable update that will be triggered is x++.

Increment and Decrement Operators

By the way, x++ is a variable assignment line. The x is the variable and the ++ is an increment operator. The function of an increment operator is to add 1 to the variable where it was placed. In this case, every time the program reads x++, the program will add 1 to the variable x. If x has a value of 10, the increment operator will change variable x's value to 11.

On the other hand, you can also use the decrement operator instead of the increment operator. The decrement operator is done by place -- next to a variable. Unlike the increment operator, the decrement subtracts 1 to its operand.

Just like the while loop, the for loop will run as long as its condition returns TRUE. However, the for loop has a built in safety measure and variable declaration. You do not need to declare the value needed for its condition outside the statement. And the safety measure to prevent infinite loop is the variable update. However, it does not mean that it will be automatically immune to infinite loops. Poor programming can lead to it. For example:

```
for (x = 1; x > 1; x++) {
    /* Insert Code Block Here */
```

```
}
```

In this example, the for loop will enter into an infinite loop unless a proper means of escape from the loop is coded inside its code block.

The structure of the for loop example is almost the same with while loop. The only difference is that the program is set to loop for only three times. In this case, it only allows the user to guess three times or until the value of variable x does not reach 3 or higher.

Every time the user guesses wrong, the value of x is incremented, which puts the loop closer in ending. However, in case the user guesses right, the code block of the if statement assigns a value higher than 3 to variable x in order to escape the loop and end the program.

The Do While Loop

This kind of loop is similar to the earlier-explained while loop but with a few more differences. Take a look at this example.

```
#include<stdio.h>

    int main()
    {
            int counter, howmuch;
            scanf("%d", &howmuch);
            counter = 0;
            do
```

```
    {
        counter++;
        printf("%d\n", counter);
    }
    while ( counter < howmuch);
    return 0;
}
```

If you would take a look at the while loop, you will notice that there is only a "while" statement that provides two sets of outcomes, one that forces the program to refer back to another block of code and another that brings about the termination of the program. With the do while loop, you are adding another check at the end of a condition to keep the program from terminating. If you would incorporate a do while loop into the example of the while loop, it would look like this.

```
#include <stdio.h>
int main()
{
    int some_number;
    int guess_result;
int counter;
guess_result = 0;
```

```c
printf( "Welcome to Guess the Magic Number program. \n" );
printf( "Guess the magic number to win. \n" );
printf( "You have unlimited chances to guess the number. \n" );
do
{
counter++;
printf(%d\n", counter);
}
    while (counter < guess_result) {

printf( "Guess the magic number: " );
scanf( "%d", &some_number );
    if ( some_number == 3 ) {
        printf( "You guessed the right number! \n" );
        guess_result = 1;
    }
    else if ( some_number > 3 ){
        printf( "Your guess is too high! \n" );
        guess_result = 0;
    }
    else {
        printf( "Your guess is too low! \n" );
        guess_result = 0;
```

```
        }
}
printf( "Thank you for playing. Press Enter to exit this program."
);
getchar();
return 0;
}
```

The main difference here is that instead of just having the cycle loop until one guesses the number, the user now has a limited number of chances to guess the magic number because of the do while statement.

The Break and Continue

Another looping method you can use in C is known as the break and continue. Take a look at the following example.

```
#include<stdio.h>

        int main()
        {
                int i;

                i = 0;
                while ( i < 20 )
                {
                i++;
                if ( i == 10)
                break;
                }
                return 0;
```

```
}
```

This represents the basic syntax of a break. You will notice that it is inside a loop in itself. In most cases, the break and continue method is mostly considered as a way to break out of loops instead of creating them.

The main premise of the loop shows that the program will continue to operate as long as the value of i is lower than twenty. Based on the way that the program has been designed, that might take a while. In order to break from the loop and give a sense of termination to the program, another if condition will be used.

```
if ( i == 10)
break;
```

This snippet of code will terminate the program because it adds another condition that stops the operation of the code.

Chapter 7: Pointers, Arrays

Now that you're getting closer to fully understanding how C programming works, it's time that you get acquainted with the more complicated elements that give C language the dynamic range it provides many programmers.

Pointers

In the realm of C language, pointers are considered as valuable pathways to memory banks of data and other variables that programmers need to access several times within the code. In other cases, pointers can direct the machine to repeatedly access a certain set of data and use them again and again without having to write down the individual elements within the code. Think of them as shortcuts to already-stored memory within your code.

Instead of using functions in order to work, pointers are used with two symbols: the asterisk (*) and the ampersand (&).

Take a look at the following example:

```
#include <stdio.h>
int main()
{
  int* pc;
  int c;
```

```
c=22;
printf("Address of c:%d\n",&c);
printf("Value of c:%d\n\n",c);
pc=&c;
printf("Address of pointer pc:%d\n",pc);
printf("Content of pointer pc:%d\n\n",*pc);
c=11;
printf("Address of pointer pc:%d\n",pc);
printf("Content of pointer pc:%d\n\n",*pc);
*pc=2;
printf("Address of c:%d\n",&c);
printf("Value of c:%d\n\n",c);
return 0;
}
```

You will notice that the function int under the line of code containing "main" is immediately followed by an asterisk. By doing so, you have designated the variable pc as a pointer.

Running this program will show you sets of information pertaining to the addresses and the values for both the variables pc and c. In the middle of each set, new statements are made to show what kind of relationship lies in between the two variables.

Address of c: 2686784

Value of c: 22

Address of pointer pc: 2686784

Content of pointer pc: 22

Address of pointer pc: 2686784

Content of pointer pc: 11

Address of c: 2686784

Value of c: 2

This is what the earlier source code will generate. Take note that the address of both c and pc do not change. This is because memory addresses used in code do not necessarily have to change, only the content of the memory address changes.

If you'll notice in the earlier sections of the code, the value of the variable c was declared to be 22. That is why the first set of displayed lines of the program will show the address of the variable c and the actual content which is 22.


```
printf("Address of c:%d\n",&c);
  printf("Value of c:%d\n\n",c);
```

Take note that in order to show the memory address of the variable c, you would have to precede it with the ampersand, right after the %d and quotation marks. Since the variable c was not listed as a pointer, the machine had no other choice but to show the direct memory address of the variable.

```
pc=&c;
   printf("Address of pointer pc:%d\n",pc);
   printf("Content of pointer pc:%d\n\n",*pc);
```

On the other hand, by declaring pc as a pointer by adding an asterisk, you can use it to refer to another value. In the example above, after declaring pc as a pointer, the value of pc was set as "&c" in the line pc=&c. By doing so, referring to *pc in any other line of code would access the memory address of the variable pc. Since the content of the memory address was a referenced as &c, then the value of c would show, which was 22.

Another thing to note is that in order to get the address of pc, you didn't have to use ampersand. This is because you've already designated the variable pc as a pointer by using an asterisk whereas the variable c was not declared as a pointer.

```
*pc=2;
   printf("Address of c:%d\n",&c);
```

```
printf("Value of c:%d\n\n",c);
```

This particular line of code changes the content of the memory address. Here you see that the variable pointer pc now has a specific value assigned to it. Since the value of "pc" was just set to "&c" and "*pc" was set to 2, the machine will still use the same memory address for the variable c but will find another value instead of 22. This is because the value of the pointer pc was changed. That would also change the value of c, which was what *pc was originally pointing to.

Arrays

Think of Arrays as an extension of pointers. With pointers, you are only using one variable as a memory address. This limits the amount of things you can reference in your code. With arrays, you have larger sets of data to play around with. That will come extremely handy when dealing with large and complex programs.

Arrays are divided into two main categories: one-dimensional and multi-dimensional arrays. Fortunately, you can declare the presence of an array in your code the same way that you declare variables, with a slight addition:

```
int sample_array[array_size]
```

This line of code will introduce the set of data you plan to use for your code. You will start with the int function and then name your array. Follow that with square brackets that enclose how many pieces of data your set contains.

After you name your array, you will have to list the elements that are inside this array. It can be done like this:

int sample[5] = {1000.0, 2.0, 3.4, 7.0, 50.0};

Start with a curly brace and then enumerate each element of your array. Separate each entry with a comma and end with another brace. Each element in that array will be assigned with a specific position. This will give each element a unique identifier that you can access within your code.

One way to make use of arrays in your programs is by having the user dictate the content of your array. Take a look at this example:

```c
#include <stdio.h>
int main(){
    int marks[10],i,n,sum=0;
    printf("Enter number of samples: ");
    scanf("%d",&n);
```

```
for(i=0;i<n;++i){
    printf("Enter value of sample%d: ",i+1);
    scanf("%d",&marks[i]);
    sum+=marks[i];
}
printf("Sum= %d",sum);
return 0;
}
```

Running this source code will prompt the user to first indicate the number of samples they're working with. After determining the number of samples, the user is asked to assign a value to each sample. Once the user has assigned a value to all of the slots in the array, the program automatically adds all of the values together and presents the sum.

You will notice that the name of the array is "marks". This identifies the array as it is to be used within the rest of the code. It is followed by the maximum number of allowable entries it can handle. Despite asking the user to determine the size of their array, it is important to declare the limit so that the code does not return any errors.

```
for(i=0;i<n;++i){
        printf("Enter value of sample%d: ",i+1);
```

```
scanf("%d",&marks[i]);
```

In this bit of code from the example, you will notice the "for" loop method being used to avoid an infinite number of entries requested from the user. The block of code under this loop is the portion that asks the user to input the values of the array that they want to use.

Multi-dimensional Arrays

The earlier example of an array was linear. Imagine having the machine lay out all the data you've set in front of you in a straight line. That is why it's called linear.

On the other hand, multi-dimensional arrays set your data across more than one dimension and creates a sort of "table" of data to present when the source code is compiled. Take a look at this example.

```
#include <stdio.h>
int main()
{
  int x;
  int y;
  int array[8][8];
```

```
for ( x = 0; x < 8; x++ ) {
  for ( y = 0; y < 8; y++ )
    array[x][y] = x * y;
}
printf( "Array Indices:\n" );
for ( x = 0; x < 8;x++ ) {
  for ( y = 0; y < 8; y++ )
  {
    printf( "[%d][%d]=%d", x, y, array[x][y] );
  }
  printf( "\n" );
}
getchar();
}
```

Notice that the declaration of the array has two sizes indicated. Both of the sizes have the same value set at 8. Each size represents the extension of that array in a particular direction, beginning horizontally and then vertically. This will generate a square composed of data entries from the array.

```
for ( x = 0; x < 8; x++ ) {
  for ( y = 0; y < 8; y++ )
    array[x][y] = x * y;
```

This block of code from the example shows a loop that works like a multiplication table. The machine multiplies the x and y variables until they reach a certain limit. This is also another application of the increment and decrement operatives from earlier.

Chapter 8: P Strings, Structures, Unions and Typedef

Now that you have a considerable amount of exposure to the coding programs using integers, it's time to include characters into the mix.

Similar to arrays , strings operate the same way, it's just that they work with characters. This especially becomes useful when you need to have your user enter specific input into your program. Take a look at this example.

```
#include <stdio.h>
int main(){
   char name[30],ch;
   int i=0;
   printf("Enter name: ");
   while(ch!='\n')
   {
      ch=getchar();
      name[i]=ch;
      i++;
   }
   name[i]='\0';
```

```
printf("Name: %s",name);
return 0;
}
```

When this code is run, it will ask the user to enter a name. This could be any name as long as the amount of characters within that name does not go beyond the 30-character limit. The declaration for the string is indicated as such:

char name[30]

You will notice that this is similar to the format of an array. Instead of using the usual int function, we use the char function which is also provided by the <stdio.h> derivative at the beginning of the code.

You've also set a variable i to help count the number of characters. The increment operative indicated further below the code will limit the input and the while(ch!='\n') portion will immediately grasp the user input as soon as they press the enter key. When this happens, the program will display the input on a separate line, minus some of the characters that have come after the user hit the space bar.

An interesting feature of strings is the name[i]='\o' appearance near the end of the source code. This indicates a null set \o which is considered part of the string. This feature acts as a terminator for the set, meaning that there is nothing left that follows.

Concatenate Strings

The program above simply displays the content of the string that the user provides. This is a very simple yet somewhat meaningless thing to do. One way to add variation to this feature is by concatenating two strings. This is known as the process of combining two strings into one sequence. Take a look at the following example.

```
#include <stdio.h>
int main()
{
    char s1[100], s2[100], i, j;
    printf("Enter first string: ");
    scanf("%s",s1);
    printf("Enter second string: ");
    scanf("%s",s2);
    for(i=0; s1[i]!='\o'; ++i);
    for(j=0; s2[j]!='\o'; ++j, ++i)
```

```
{
    s1[i]=s2[j];
}
s1[i]='\0';
printf("After concatenation: %s",s1);
return 0;
}
```

This program will ask the user to enter characters for two different sets. Once the user enters input for both sets, the machine puts them together in one sequence. You will notice that two strings have been put together in a single display line, as if completing a sentence. The machine will take the string input from both sources and lay them out in a linear fashion, similar to adding the two statements together.

Structures

Much of the content you've covered so far deals with sets of data an input of the same kind. Pointers and arrays are meant for integer-only groups while strings are for character-only sets of input.

Structures, on the other hand, are used to contain data from different types of input for easier access within the code. A good application of such a function can be found when filling up a profile of a particular person. By using a structure, you can combine their age, address, name and other variables into one collective element to represent that person. Take a look at this example:

```c
#include <stdio.h>
#include <string.h>

struct Books
{
   char  title[50];
   char  author[50];
   char  subject[100];
   int   book_id;
};

int main( )
{
   struct Books Book1;
   struct Books Book2;
```

```c
strcpy( Book1.title, "C Programming");
strcpy( Book1.author, "Nuha Ali");
strcpy( Book1.subject, "C Programming Tutorial");
Book1.book_id = 6495407;

strcpy( Book2.title, "Telecom Billing");
strcpy( Book2.author, "Zara Ali");
strcpy( Book2.subject, "Telecom Billing Tutorial");
Book2.book_id = 6495700;

printf( "Book 1 title : %s\n", Book1.title);
printf( "Book 1 author : %s\n", Book1.author);
printf( "Book 1 subject : %s\n", Book1.subject);
printf( "Book 1 book_id : %d\n", Book1.book_id);

printf( "Book 2 title : %s\n", Book2.title);
printf( "Book 2 author : %s\n", Book2.author);
printf( "Book 2 subject : %s\n", Book2.subject);
printf( "Book 2 book_id : %d\n", Book2.book_id);

return 0;
}
```

The example above creates two separate structures, namely, Book1 and Book2. You've also probably noticed a new directive included in the beginning of the code.

#include <string.h>

This line includes the <string.h> library into your code which will allow you to use the function "strcpy" which is a shorter version of string copy. Using this function tells the machine the obtain the data from a particular element within your structure when you need to reference it after your declaration.

You will also notice that referencing the string data from an entry requires a different syntax, namely "%s" instead of the "%d" used for integers. As seen in this snippet of code below.

```
printf( "Book 1 title : %s\n", Book1.title);
printf( "Book 1 author : %s\n", Book1.author);
printf( "Book 1 subject : %s\n", Book1.subject);
printf( "Book 1 book_id : %d\n", Book1.book_id);
```

This chunk of code is responsible for this display when the code is run.

Book 1 title : C Programming

Book 1 author : Nuha Ali

Book 1 subject : C Programming Tutorial

Book 1 book_id : 6495407

Look at how the last display line contains both strings and integers in one line. This shows how structures enable users to mix in different types of data groups into one classification without having to create several different variables in multiple declarations. It saves programmers a lot of time when it comes to programming.

Unions

Apart from structures, unions are another way to group different data types into one memory address. Take a look at the following example.

```
#include <stdio.h>
#include <string.h>

union Data
{
  int i;
  float f;
```

```c
  char str[20];
};

int main( )
{
  union Data data;

  data.i = 10;
  printf( "data.i : %d\n", data.i);

  data.f = 220.5;
  printf( "data.f : %f\n", data.f);

  strcpy( data.str, "C Programming");
  printf( "data.str : %s\n", data.str);

  return 0;
}
```

This set of code will generate the following lines of display

data.i : 10

data.f : 220.500000

data.str : C Programming

You would notice that unions are constructed the same way as structures. The main difference between the two is that structures have different memory addresses for each of the members inside of it. Unions, on the other hand, only hold one memory address that contains all of the members. In order to use the individual items within the union, you would need a separate declaration of which member you want to access such as this.

```
data.i = 10;
  printf( "data.i : %d\n", data.i);
```

Typedef

You would notice in the examples that we've had so far that the variables we use belong to a specific type of data input. It could be an integer or a character. Later on within this book you will also encounter other data types that you can use within your codes.

Despite being limited to the kinds of data types you can use, you can actually dictate a new type of data and assign it to a variable. This is known as a typedef. To understand how it works in detail, take a look at the following example.

```
#include <stdio.h>
#include <string.h>
```

```c
typedef struct Books
{
   char  title[50];
   char  author[50];
   char  subject[100];
   int   book_id;
} Book;

int main( )
{
   Book book;

   strcpy( book.title, "C Programming");
   strcpy( book.author, "Nuha Ali");
   strcpy( book.subject, "C Programming Tutorial");
   book.book_id = 6495407;

   printf( "Book title : %s\n", book.title);
   printf( "Book author : %s\n", book.author);
   printf( "Book subject : %s\n", book.subject);
   printf( "Book book_id : %d\n", book.book_id);

   return 0;
```

```
}
```

You will notice that the typedef function in the earlier sections of the code introduced a new type of data known as Books. The Books variable was assigned as a structure that contained different members. By assigning the variable Books via typedef, you can now reference the various members of the structure by using the variable Books as shown here:

```
strcpy( book.title, "C Programming");
  strcpy( book.author, "Nuha Ali");
  strcpy( book.subject, "C Programming Tutorial");
  book.book_id = 6495407;
```

You will notice that you no longer have to use the term struct to reference your structure. Instead, you simply use Books since you used tyedef to assign Books to represent the structure. By executing the code above, you will get the following display.

Book title : C Programming
Book author : Nuha Ali
Book subject : C Programming Tutorial
Book book_id : 6495407

Typedef provides another way through which you can assign your variable if in case you're already using many types of data input. It also prevents you from getting confused when you are typing in long codes for larger programs.

Chapter 9: The other Header Files

So far, the programs and codes you have been dealing with contained the standard header #include at the beginning of the code. This statement allows us to use the <stdio.h> library to use functions such as printf and scanf. In the earlier chapter, you encountered a new inclusion which was <string.h> which gave you access to the strctcpy function. The files <stdio.h> and <string.h> are known as header files and they are declared at the beginning of you code to delineate the functions and variables that you can use within your program.

As you might have noticed, there is a vast number of header files available for use. On top of that, different compilers have their own set of header files that a programmer can use. Some header files do not work on some compilers. A good example would be the header file <graphic.h>. This header file contains shapes and figures that can be used to form pictures instead of text for a program. Unfortunately, this header file does not work with some compilers such as Code::Blocks as it was developed for Turbo C. When you attempt larger and more elaborate programs, you'll find more header files with functions that will suit your needs. For a meantime, we only need to understand a few more of the basic header files in order to add more dimensions to your program.

<string.h>

Just as the file name implies, this header file allows you to take action on your strings. Another inclusion in this header are the structure-specific functions such as strcpy. You will remember that the strcpy function takes the original content of one of the strings in a structure so that you could use it with a printf function. There are other functions within the <string.h> header that you can use with strings. Take a look at this example.

```c
#include <stdio.h>
#include <string.h>

int main()
{
  char a[100], b[100];

  printf("Enter the first string\n");
  gets(a);

  printf("Enter the second string\n");
```

```
gets(b);

if( strcmp(a,b) == 0 )
    printf("Entered strings are equal.\n");
else
    printf("Entered strings are not equal.\n");

return 0;
}
```

If you run this code, it will prompt the user to provide two strings. If the user places a space in between any of the characters, then the rest is not recorded. Once the user enters the two strings, the program will tell you if both strings are equal or not.

strcmp

This is the function that does the comparison. Naturally, it has been named strcmp. It takes the value of both of the strings and returns a value depending on the outcome. In the example above, the strcmp function was designed to return the value of 0 if the value of the strings are equal. The if statement is then followed by the printf function declaring that the strings were equal. The else statement was created to display the opposite if in the case that strcmp did not return zero.

You will also notice the inclusion of a new function in this code, the "get" function. In C language, the get function works the same way as the scanf function. It provides programmers with an easier alternative for obtaining input from the user. This function is also part of the <stdio.h> header file and can be used interchangeable with the scanf function.

strcat

The <string.h> function also has a shortcut function for lining two separate strings together into one line of display. You will remember that this process is called concatenating strings. You can also do this with the strcat function. Take a look at the example.

```
#include <stdio.h>
#include <string.h>

int main()
{
  char a[100], b[100];
```

```
printf("Enter the first string\n");
gets(a);

printf("Enter the second string\n");
gets(b);

strcat(a,b);

printf("String obtained on concatenation is %s\n",a);

return 0;
}
```

The beginning of the code shows that two strings are being identified, each with a limit of 100 characters. Each of these declarations are followed by a gets function to obtain input from the user. Following the gets functions was the strcat function. Take note that the value placed within the function combines the aptly-named strings a and b.

Instead of using more lines of code within the earlier example of concatenating strings with pointers, you can simply use the strcat function to line them up.

There are programmers who choose to combine their lines using pointers instead of the strcat function. This is because they already have a mastery of pointers and are well-aware of their applications within C. You will also find other functions that can be substituted with the use of pointers as you learn more about programming. You can use either pointers and functions to do what you need because your compiler recognizes both methods.

strlen

Another function that comes with the <string.h> header is the ability to compute for the length of a string. This can be done with the strlen function. Observe the following example.

```c
#include <stdio.h>
#include <string.h>
int main ()
{
   char str[50];
   int len;
printf("enter text to be measured here \n");
   gets(str);
   len = strlen(str);
   printf("Length of |%s| is |%d|\n", str, len);
```

```
    return(o);
}
```

This code will ask the user to enter a string of characters to be measured. Take note that we are now using the gets function to obtain input from the user to make it easier.

After declaring the string and the integer representation for the length of the string, using the strlen gets the length of the input and stores that data. Using the printf function allows you to draw that value and display it in a separate line of code. When the user is done entering the string on the program, it will return with the amount of characters within the string.

One thing to take note of, though, is that strings will always have one extra character to terminate their lengths. This is known as the null set. When setting limits on your strings, be sure to account for then null set at the end of your string by adding 1 to your total number. The example above can only accommodate 49 characters in total on account of the null set taking then 50th slot.

<time.h>

Another interesting header file available in C is the <time.h> file. Naturally, this gives you access to different functions that manipulate the time settings on your computer and few more interesting time frames from other points. Take a look at this example.

```
#include <stdio.h>
#include <time.h>
int main ()
{
    time_t sec;
    sec = time ();

    printf ("Number of hours since January 1, 1970 is %ld \n",
sec/3600);
    return 0;
}
```

When this code is run, it will only display a single line of text saying the number of hours since January January 1, 1970 based on your computers' clock.

You might be wondering what the significance of January 1, 1970 is in relation to C programming. You will be surprised to know that the first UNIX computer system became operable on that same date. This is known as the "Big Bang" for computers. The time mentioned in the example is called UNIX time.

Take note that you would first have to declare the variable sec with the time_t function. This function introduces a variable that will pull out data from the time register within the machine. Simply using int in this case will no longer work if you want to display the time and date from a specific point.

```
time_t sec;
  sec = time ();
```

The null set next to time in the above snippet of code retrieves the time that has passed since the Big Bang for computers.

Ctime

Instead of using UNIX time as a reference point, you can also use the standard point in time right now using the time function. Observe the following example.

```
#include <time.h>
#include <stdio.h>
```

```
int main(void)
{
time_t mytime;
mytime = time();
printf(ctime(&mytime));

return 0;
}
```

This code will produce a single display line that shows the current local time for your area based your machine. Notice that the ctime function was not declared immediately in this example as this is already a known function within the compiler.

The time_t function relays the time into a variable. When you give the variable a value such as time(), that will prompt the system to display the current date and time within this format: www mmm dd hh:mm:ss yyyy. This means it will show first the day of the week, followed by the month, the date, the hour, minutes, seconds and the current year. Most programmers use this function to display the time wherein their codes were created for credit purposes.

<math.h>

Despite having created a simple calculator program in the earlier chapters, your calculator would need a lot more functions to become more useful. Although incorporating all the four basic operations was tricky enough to do, there is another header file that can give you access to more complicated procedures in math which is the <math.h>. Follow the example below.

```c
#include <stdio.h>
#include <math.h>

int main()
{
  int n, result;

  printf("Enter an integer to calculate it's absolute value\n");
  scanf("%d", &n);

  result = abs(n);

  printf("Absolute value of %d = %d\n", n, result);

  return 0;
```

}

abs

This set of code, when executed, will ask the user to input an integer, regardless if it is positive or negative. Once the user hits the enter key, the program will return the absolute value of the user input. This is what the abs function is for, which is short for absolute. Be careful to notice that in order to use the abs function, you would need to include the <math.h> header file at the beginning along with the <stdio.h> file in order to get all the functions that you need.

Of course, finding the absolute value of an integer is easy enough done alone without the help of a program. The math.h header file also has more complex operations at hand. Take a look at the following example.

```
#include <stdio.h>
#include <math.h>

int main()
{
  double c, d, result;
```

```
printf("Enter c and d to calculate c^d\n");
scanf("%lf%lf", &c, &d);

result = pow(c, d);

printf("%.2lf raised to %.2lf = %.2lf\n", c, d, result);

return 0;
}
```

pow

The above code will generate a computation for two variables that you combine. The variable c will be the base of the equation and the variable d is considered the exponent or power to which you'll be raising the base. The pow function can be found as a value for the variable result.

You will also notice some changes within your code, namely, the absence of the int variables and the presence of a new type which is double.

By the way, there are different ways through which you can introduce your variables into your code. The function int is the most widely used but it is limited because it cannot store decimal places. It can only store whole numbers.

On the other hand, there are floating data types that you can use to contain values that have decimal places. The "double" function you see in the code is an example of a floating data-type. Take note that all the variables can be expressed in decimals because they were all included within the double classification. If you had used an int function, the program would have returned an error to you.

To use the pow function, be sure to delineate which two of your variables you plan to use in a specific order. Start with your base followed by the exponent. That is how the machine will read your command. After the user provides the values of c and d for the program, it will return with the result which is c multiplied to itself d times.

sqrt

Although this may sound a bit funny, the sqrt function allows you to extract the sqare root of a given value. Take a look at the following example.

```
#include <stdio.h>
#include <math.h>

int main()
{
  double n, result;

  printf("Enter a number to calculate it's square root\n");
  scanf("%lf", &n);

  result = sqrt(n);

  printf("Square root of %.2lf = %.2lf\n", n, result);

  return 0;
}
```

Notice that you're once again using floating data types in the form of double variables. Remember that square roots are often expressed in long decimal points instead of whole numbers.

Another thing to notice is that you don't necessarily have to find the symbol of the square root in order to use the sqrt function. All you have to do is to declare on which floating variable you want to use the function.

log

You can attempt even more complicated processes by using the log function. Naturally, this function extracts the natural logarithm of a number, using the base e. For the beginner, the natural logarithm for any number is the results of raising the base e to the number itself. The base e is a mathematical constant set at 2.718281...

This program below shows a sample program that extracts the natural logarithm of a number.

```
#include <stdio.h>
#include <math.h>

int main()
{
  double n, result;

  printf("Enter a number to calculate it's natural log (base is e)\n");
```

```
scanf("%lf", &n);

result = log(n);

printf("Natural log of %.2lf = %lf\n", n, result);

return 0;
}
```

Again, notice the inclusion of the <math.h> header file. This will give you access to the log and pow functions.

Chapter 10: Command Line Arguments, Recursion and Binary Files

With the experience and practice that you've had from programming with C, you've mostly dealt with the nitty-gritty of the code and less with the other lines of code found on the top. This chapter will help you get acquainted with some of the symbols on top that you might have been wondering about.

Command Line Arguments

You have learned from this book that your programs should start with a main() line before you start declaring your variables and functions. This is standard practice that most beginners just pass off as a simple rule. But the main() function can also have values and parameters placed within the parentheses. These are known as arguments.

When you place arguments within your main() declaration, you will end up with a command line through which the user can modify the program from the outside instead of going back into the nitty-gritty of the code. These are command line arguments. Take a look at this example.

```c
#include <stdio.h>
int main( int argc, char *argv[] )
{
  printf("Program name %s\n", argv[0]);
  if( argc == 2 )
  {
    printf("The argument supplied is %s\n", argv[1]);
  }
  else if( argc > 2 )
  {
    printf("Too many arguments supplied.\n");
  }
  else
  {
    printf("One argument expected.\n");
  }
}
```

By running this code, the console will display a result depending on how many arguments you have in your command line. The machine will most likely turn up with "one argument expected" because your whole program is simply a calculation of the arguments in the code. Now let us add a more specific action within the code. Take a look at this one.

```c
#include <stdio.h>
int main ( int argc, char *argv[] )
{
  if ( argc != 2 )
  {
    printf( "usage: %s filename", argv[0] );
  }
  else
  {
    FILE *file = fopen( argv[1], "r" );

    if ( file == 0 )
    {
      printf( "Could not open file\n" );
    }
    else
    {
      int x;
      while  ( ( x = fgetc( file ) ) != EOF )
      {
        printf( "%c", x );
```

```
        }
      fclose( file );
    }
  }
```

This code prompts your computer to access a certain file. Given that there is no such file on your computer, the program will return a message saying "could not open file". On the other hand, if your machine did have the file, the program would open each character in the file and display it on the screen until the end of the file itself.

In order to incorporate command line arguments into your code, you would need to introduce some parameters into the main() declaration, namely:

main (int argc, char *argv[])

In this line of code, the int argc portion refers to the number of arguments you place within the program and the char *argv[]

represents a pointer that leads to an array arguments to which to compare the argc parameter. It may seem a little difficult to understand at first but it serves a very important purpose.

As mentioned earlier, command line arguments allow your programs to tell you if there is something wrong after you have them executed. Instead of going into the code to hard-wire everything, the program will tell you what is wrong via the console. This in turn, will make it easier for you to locate the bug and fix your problem.

Recursion

Another interesting feature of C programming is having functions perform functions within themselves, or rather, declaring functions within functions. This is known as recursion. In order to get a clear idea on how this works, take a look at the following example.

```c
#include <stdio.h>

int main()

int fibonaci(int i)

{
  if(i == 0)

  {
    return 0;

  }
  if(i == 1)

  {
    return 1;

  }
```

```
   return fibonaci(i-1) + fibonaci(i-2);
}
int main()
{
   int i;
   for (i = 0; i < 10; i++)
   {
     printf("%d\t%n", fibonaci(i));
   }
   return 0;
}
```

Take note that the variable has been named Fibonaci, does this sound familiar? Also known as one of the more interesting facets of mathematics, a Fibonacci sequence is linear representation of numbers that follow a unique pattern. This pattern is simply the result of the two preceding numbers. The example above is a program that will initiate a Fibonacci sequence when run.

The program will display the numbers 1, 1, 2, 3, 5, 8 in order. This is the most basic Fibonacci sequence starting with the number 1.

```
   return fibonaci(i-1) + fibonaci(i-2);
```

This statement above shows the recursive function in the program. It adds two values while adding two more values within each addend. Most programming schools use the Fibonacci sequence to illustrate recursive functions.

But the most practical aspect of recursive functions lie within a more complicated and helpful feature allowed on C, Binary Trees.

Binary Trees

Besides checking your work and setting parameters to your code, more complicated C programs make use of something known as binary trees.

From the term itself, binary trees are structured forms of information that stem from an original parent. This is called a parent node. From the parent node, two smaller child nodes branch out into the left and right. Each node is aptly named the left child node and the right child node.

Before diving into the code part of Binary trees, it is important to understand how they are represented. Imagine having the one parent element or key value known as X.

X

Your binary tree shall start out as such. With that image in mind, try extending the tree by making branch out into the left and right sides, each side with another value different than X.

X

/\

(x>c)   (x<c)

With that image in mind, you'll notice that the new branches have different values in relation to X. The left node c, contains a value that is greater than X while the right node c contains a value that is larger than X. This is how a binary tree operates within the C language. Each parent node contains something that is known as a key_value that is supposed to be declared. From the parent key_value, the left and right branches contain values that are respectively lower and higher than the original key_value of X.

Using trees in C programming allows users to create a simple yet efficient model through which they can insert elements, find elements and even delete their elements. Take a look at this example.

```c
#include<stdlib.h>
#include<stdio.h>

struct tree_el {
    int val;
    struct tree_el * right, * left;
};
typedef struct tree_el node;
void insert(node ** tree, node * item) {
    if(!(*tree)) {
        *tree = item;
        return;
    }
    if(item->val<(*tree)->val)
        insert(&(*tree)->left, item);
    else if(item->val>(*tree)->val)
        insert(&(*tree)->right, item);
}

void printout(node * tree) {
```

```
  if(tree->left) printout(tree->left);
  printf("%d\n",tree->val);
  if(tree->right) printout(tree->right);
}


void main() {
  node * curr, * root;
  int i;
  root = NULL;
  for(i=1;i<=10;i++) {
    curr = (node *)malloc(sizeof(node));
    curr->left = curr->right = NULL;
    curr->val = rand();
    insert(&root, curr);
  }
  printout(root);
}
```

This code, when run, will display a list of numbers on several lines. This represents the structure of the binary tree. The numbers on the lines represent amounts of information stored in each child node.

Take note that there was a new header file used which was <stdlib.h> This header file allows us to use certain functions that instruct the machine to place data in the form of a binary tree that has two child nodes branching out from the parent node.

Knowledge on Binary trees is going to play an important role in helping you prepapre for more aggressive and complicated programs through the C programming language. Remember that this book only covers the basics which will serve as a foundation to help you master the language and move on to more complicated programming   methods.

Chapter 11: File Handling – Creating and Opening Files

Creating files that can be saved on a storage device (such as a hard drive, a USB pen drive, or some other external storage) will greatly enhance your programming skills. It increases the usefulness of any software system that you create. A lot of computer programs make use of files for a lot of different reasons. Files can serve as records of the processes that have been performed by a program you wrote.

The C programming language allows you to create a file, open any file that exists on storage, read the data stored in those files, write any necessary data into said files that have been opened, and close a file after all processes have been performed. This programming language allows your programs to handle both binary files (i.e. system oriented data) as well as text files (i.e. stream oriented data).

System Oriented vs. Stream Oriented Data Files

Text data files are usually called stream oriented data while binary files are also called system oriented data. Sometimes you get to wonder how these two terms differ. The following are quick and easy definitions:

Stream oriented data in C language refers to any form of data that is stored just the way you see it on a console (i.e. your computer screen). When you use this type of data file everything else takes place automatically. This means that data conversions, buffering, as well as input and output operations become automatic.

System oriented data on the other hand doesn't work that way. Files or data that is system oriented are the ones that an operating system usually works on. Well, they're called binary files simply because you're dealing with strings of ones and zeroes. This type of data is usually stored first in a computer's memory. This type of data doesn't have to be translated into text for it to be stored on your hard drive or external storage.

File Creation and Manipulation Process in C Language

There are five steps in order to create, access, and make changes to files that are kept in storage. They are the following:

1. Use a pointer variable to declare a file.
2. Open the created or a file that is already on disk. The fopen library function is used just for that.
3. Use any suitable function in order to manipulate and process the data stored in a file (or files). You will need to use read and write functions in this step.
4. Close the file. To close a file, use the fclose() function.

Functions in C That You Can Use for File Handling

The following are the functions that you can use in order to handle a file. Note that a lot of these are input and output functions. There is no need to use any other header since these functions are all available in the standard input/output library (i.e. stdio).

- fopen – This is used to open a file.
- feof – This function is for the end of file marker.
- fputs – This one is used to write a character string.
- fgets – This one reads a character string.

- fscanf – This is the function used for any formatted input coming from a file.
- fprintf – This one is for writing or saving any formatted output to a file.
- putw – This one is used to write an integer to a file.
- getw – This is the function you'll use to read integers.
- putc – This one is used to write a character instead of a string.
- getc – This one is used to read a character instead of a string.
- fclose – This one is the opposite of the fopen function – it closes a specified file.

The fopen Function in C

It is obvious that you cannot read data from or write data to a file that doesn't exist. In C language and other programming languages out there, you also need to open a file that already exists in storage first before you can make use of any data stored in it. In order to perform both functions, you will need to use the fopen function.

The syntax for this function is as follows:

file *fopen(const char * filename, const char * mode);

That is the the standard syntax you'll find in many documentations and program code in C language. The following are the parameters used in the above mentioned syntax:

- filename – This part of the syntax will be a literal string argument. You will be specifying a specific directory where the file is located, so to speak. Consider the following sample:

fp=fopen("c:\\sample.txt", "r");

Note that you need to use double backslashes (i.e. "\\") to identify a directory. In the example above, you're referring to the root directory of a drive "c:" which is where the sample.txt file is located. Don't worry too much about the double backslashes; that's just the way C language handles quoted strings. It basically helps compilers distinguish this code with the "\" key.

- mode – This is the argument that will define the type of access mode.

This function uses a pointer data structure (please review the discussion of pointers mentioned in this book if needed). It points to a file that needs to be opened or a file that will be created. Given the syntax of the fopen function, you can see that it gives a value to the pointer which points to a file. This pointer allows the program to keep track of the file being used. Think of it as a type of memory address that identifies the existence of a file. Once the file is opened, the FILE pointer will allow the compiler to perform various functions. The program can then perform both read and write functions on the file that was opened.

Access Modes

As you can see from the code above, there is a second argument in the syntax of the fopen function. That second argument refers to the access mode that fopen() will use. The syntax will only accept six possible entries, which are the following:

a+	This access mode opens a file that already exists in the drive path expressed in the first argument. If that file does not exist then this function will create the file using the name provided in the "filename" argument. This also means that reading any data will begin at the start of the file but any data to be added can only be appended at the end.
w+	This mode also creates a file if it does not yet exist in the drive path

	provided in the initial argument. It also opens any existing file both for reading and writing data. If the file already exists in the drive, any data contained in it will be erased when you use this switch.
r+	This switch will open a file that is already on the drive for reading and writing.
a	This access mode also creates a file if it does not exist in the indicated drive path. However, this switch will only open a file for appending, which means any new data will only be added at the end of the file.
w	This access mode only opens a file for writing. If the file does not exist in the drive, then a new file will be created.
r	This access mode only opens an existing text file.

Errors and Possible Return Values

As you write your codes in C language, you may sometimes enter the wrong switches or strings in either the "mode" or "filename" arguments. One common error is using a value for the access mode that does not create a file. Another possible error is when a user specifies a file name and your program tries to open it and doesn't find in on the drive. Other errors can be caused by a write protected file and other possible conditions. If the file does not exist, an error occurs, or the process returns a failure then the fopen() function returns a NULL. However, if the function is a success, then it result in a file stream pointer.

Here's a sample code using fopen().

```
#include<stdio.h>

int main()

{

    FILE *fp;
```

```
fp = fopen("c:\\thisisatest.txt","w");
return 0;

}
```

This example will create a file in the root directory of drive "c:" with a file name of thisisatest.txt. Since the code includes a "w" for the access mode then a new file will be created in case it doesn't yet exist in the drive. The file that is opened or created will then be ready for writing new data.

Chapter 12: File Reading and Writing Data

You have seen how a new file is created in C language. Along with the sample codes provided and the syntax of the fopen() function, you have also learned how to open files for reading, writing, and appending. In this chapter we'll look into the other file access functions included in the standard input/output library.

Closing a File

All files that have been opened needs to be closed. Remember that fopen() opens a memory stream and that needs to be released since it is a resource that should also be usable by other programs if it is no longer needed by the one you created. To release any memory stream opened by the fopen function, you should include an fclose function at the end of your code after all file processes have been completed.

The fclose Function

The fclose() function has the following declaration:

int fclose(FILE * stream);

If the fclose() function fails then it result in an EOF. If it is successful then it gives a 0 value.

Here is a sample code that uses the fclose function.

#include<stdio.h>

int main()

```
{

    FILE *fp;
    fp = fopen("c:\\thisisatest.txt","w");
    fclose(fp);
    return 0;

}
```

The getc() Function

Another file handling function that was mentioned earlier was getc. This function reads one character from an already opened file. Note that the file should have been opened for reading. Note the following syntax:

int getc(file *stream);

If the function is successful then it returns the next object that is requested. It can also return an EOF, when all the characters in the stream have been accessed. It can also return an error in case it is unable to get a character or if something goes wrong during the process.

The following is a sample code that uses the getc() function:

```
#include<stdio.h>

int main()

{

  FILE *fp = fopen("samplefile.txt", "r");
```

```
int samk1 = getc(fp);

while (samk1 != EOF)

{

  putchar(samk1);

  ch = getc(fp);
}

if (feof(fp))

    printf("\n this is the end of the file.");

else

    printf("\n encountered error while accessing file.");

fclose(fp);

getchar();
return 0;

}
```

The putc() Function in C

You can say that the putc function is the opposite of the getc function. If getc reads a character from the specified stream then putc adds a character to the stream in the open file. This function has the following syntax:

```
int putc( int char, file *stream );
```

As you can see, this function has two arguments. The first one is for "char," which is the character that will be written to the file. Note that this will be passed to the file in its int promotion.

The other argument in this syntax is "stream." It is a pointer – you should have guessed that correctly by now by simply looking at the syntax of the code. It identifies the stream where the character in the first argument (i.e. char) should be written.

If the function results in an error then it returns an EOF. However, most of the time, it returns an unsigned character. Note that the character it will also be cast as an int.

The following is a sample code that demonstrates the use of the putc() function:

```c
#include <stdio.h>

int main ()
{
    FILE *fp;
    int xy;

    fp = fopen("sample.txt", "w");
    for( xy = 33 ; ch <= 100; xy++ )
    {
        putc(xy, fp);
    }
    fclose(fp);

    return(0);
}
```

The getw Function vs. putw Function

You can also write codes that will read and write integer data into files. The getw and the putw are two file handling functions in C that will perform the said operations. Writing integer data to file will require the putw function and reading integer data will require the getw function.

The getw function has the following syntax:

int getw(file *);

This function, obviously, returns an integer value. It has a single argument, which is "file," which actually indicates the location of the file that will be read by your program. The following is a sample code that illustrates how the getw function is used:

```
void main()

{

  FILE *fp;
  int x;

    fp = fopen("sampleintfile.txt","r");

    x = getw(fp);
    printf("%d",x);

  fclose(fp);

}
```

In this sample code, the integer value of the file sampleintfile.txt will be accessed. It will then be stored in an int variable called x. The value of x will be printed. There will be cases when the value of x will return a character when you use printf(). The character of course is the ASCII value of the int. So, don't be surprised if the output on your screen using the above code returns a letter or some other character. Check out its ASCII equivalent, that's what the code is actually showing you.

Moving on to the putw function; it has the following syntax:

int putw(integer, file*);

Unlike the getw function, putw has two arguments. The "integer" argument indicates the integer that will be written on the file. The second argument, file*, will indicate the location of the file where the new data should be added.

As you can see from the declaration above, this function will return an integer. The following is a sample code that illustrates how the putw function is used:

```
void main()

{
    FILE *fp;

    fp=fopen("sampleintfile1.txt","w");
    putw(66,fp);

    fclose(fp);
}
```

Of course, you won't see what actually happens since this code does not provide any output to the screen. What you can do to verify if your code was a success is to open sampleintfile1.txt and see if the value 66 was added. Another way to see if the code was a success is to add a printf to the code above so that the value of fp can be displayed on screen.

The fprintf Function

As stated in an earlier section of this book, fprintf returns a formatted output. The formatted output is actually sent to a stream data contained in the file. The syntax or declaration of the fprintf function is as follows:

int fprintf (file *stream, const char *format, ...)

This function has two arguments and parameters. The first parameter in the syntax above is stream; it is a pointer data structure. It identifies the file object. The other parameter in the syntax above is "format." Simply put, it is the text or the string that should be written to the indicated in the first parameter, i.e. stream.

This parameter may have embedded tags. As you can see in the syntax, the fprintf function actually waits for additional arguments, which can actually make the format of the stream more complex. The tags have the following basic structure:

%[flags][width][.precision][length]specifier

As you can see, this parameter has the following tags: flags, width, precision, and length. Let us begin with the first tag. The following are the flags that may be used in this parameter:

o	Pads the number with zeroes. The zero padding is to the left. The amount of zero pads will be specified by the sub-specifier called

113

	"width" (i.e. the tag that follows flags)
#	This forces the output to contain a decimal point. Note that if there will be no decimal added if no digits follow. This flag is used with the following specifiers: o,x, ox, X, oX, g, G, e, and E.
<space>	Inserts a blank space before the specified value if there will be no sign written.
+	Forces a + or − to precede the function's result. Note that the result is presumed positive and it will only show a negative sign when the actual output is a negative number.
-	Changes the default right justification of the output to left justification.

The following are the widths (i.e. the second tag) that may be used in this parameter:

*	Use this to that the width is not indicated. It acts as an extra integer value that precedes the actual argument that should be formatted.
<number>	Specifies the minimum amount of numbers that should be written. In case the number that should be written is shorter than the number indicated in this tag, then the number to be written will be padded with blank spaces. Note that the number will not be truncated even the actual number to be written is larger than the number specified here.

The following are the values that can be used in the .precision tag:

.*	This indicates that the precision is not specified. This acts as an extra int value argument that precedes the actual argument that needs formatting.
.number	This is used for the following integer specifiers: X, x, u, o, i, and d. This specifies what the minimum number of digits that should appear. If the actual value is larger than this precision tag, it will not be truncated. If it is shorter then it will be padded with leading zeroes. If a 0 is specified for the precision tag then no number is written. Note that all the numbers will be printed until the null character is reached. A default precision of 1 is assumed when there is no precision

	value specified. A value of 0 is assumed if only a period "." is indicated. Note that the precision can also be used with G and g specifiers, which indicates the maximum number of significant digits that should be written. It may also be used with the specifiers f, E, and e, which will indicate the number of decimal places. Finally, when used with an s specifier, this precision will indicate the total possible amount of digits that will be written.

The next tag in this parameter is length. This tag may contain the following values:

L	This tag indicates a long double. This also means that it only applies to floating point numbers.
l	This tag indicates an unsigned or long int. It works with all integer specifiers. It can also work as a specifier for wide characters, such as the case for the s and c specifiers.
h	Indicates an unsigned short int or short int. This means it works in tandem with integer specifiers.

Note that additional arguments can be made, as stated earlier. Each of the extra arguments must contain a value that should be included in the place of a tag. The rule is that there should be the same number of arguments as there are tags that are actually expecting a value to be returned.

If this function is successful, supply the characters that were written on the file. If it fails then a negative number will be returned by this function.

The following is a sample code that demonstrates the fprintf function:

```c
#include <stdio.h>
#include <stdlib.h>

int main()

{

   FILE * fp;

   fp = fopen ("sample.txt", "w+");
   fprintf(fp, "%s %s %s %d", "This", "is", "the year", 5022);

   fclose(fp);

   return(0);

}
```

The fscanf Function

The fscanf() function is the opposite of the fprintf function. Simply put, it reads any formatted data from a file. Notice that the syntax for both functions is very much alike:

int fscanf(FILE *stream, const char *format, ...)

This function also has the same parameters. The format parameter is a string. This string contains format specifiers, non-whitespace characters, and white space characters. The format argument also has tags. The stream parameter above refers to a pointer that defines a file object. This file object is also used to identify the stream.

The following are the arguments used in the fscanf function:

type	This is a character that will specify the data type that should be read from the file. It also determines which way the data should be read. There are seven type specifiers.
modifiers	This argument indicates a different size. It is used in conjunction with long doubles, doubles, unsigned long int, long int, unsigned short int, short int, float, unsigned int, and int data structures.
width	This argument simply specifies the total amount of characters that will be allowed in each time the program reads from a file.
*	This is an optional argument. When used, it signifies that data can be read from the stream; however, the data should be ignored, which means its value will not be stored in argument that corresponds to it.

The following are the type specifiers in the fscanf function:

X, x	This specifies a hexadecimal integer. Type of argument is int*
u	Specifies an unsigned integer (unsigned int*)
s	This specifies a character string. It will make the function keep on reading until white space is encountered. This is a char* type of argument. White space includes tabs, new lines, and blanks.
o	This specifies an octal integer. It is an int* type of argument.
G, g, f, E, e	This is for numbers containing decimals. These numbers may be preceded by + or - signs. This is a float* type of argument.
d	Denotes a decimal integer. It may or may not have a preceding + or - sign. It is an int* type of argument.
c	Denotes a single character to be read from file. Usually reads the next following character in the opened file. It may read width characters as well.

Just like the fprintf function, this one can also have additional arguments (see the syntax and observe the "..." at the end). The additional arguments may be included in lieu of any of the tags mentioned above. However, there should be the same number of extra arguments and tags as specified in the syntax of this function.

The following is a sample code that shows how the fscanf function is used:

```
#include <stdio.h>
#include <stdlib.h>


int main()

{
  char s1[10], s2[10], s3[10];
  int yr;
  FILE * fp;

  fp = fopen ("sample.txt", "w+");
  fputs("This is the year 5199", fp);

  rewind(fp);
  fscanf(fp, "%s %s %s %d", s1, s2, s3, &yr);

  printf("This is the first string |%s|\n", s1 );
  printf("This is the second string |%s|\n", s2 );
  printf("This is the third |%s|\n", s3 );
  printf("And this is the last entry |%d|\n", yr );

  fclose(fp);

  return(0);

}
```

The fgets Function

The fgets fuction will read a line from a stream that was specified in the declaration. That line of data will be stored in a string variable and a pointer structure will be pointing to that string. It has the following syntax:

char *fgets(char *str, int n, FILE *stream)

Note that certain conditions will stop this function from reading from file. It will stop reading when the final character is reached. It will also stop reading when it gets to the null character. It will also stop when a new line is reached. Of course, just like all functions that read from a file, when it reaches the EOF then it will also stop reading.

As you can see from the syntax, this library function has three different parameters. The first one is *str. Judging by the syntax, this refers to a pointer data structure. It points to an array of characters where the string that was read from file is stored.

The next parameter in the syntax is n, which is an integer. It represents the total number of character that should be read. This maximum value will include the null character. The length of the array is used to determine this value. The last parameter is *stream, which is a pointer that refers to a file object.

Return Value

If the fgets function gives back a null pointer when it encounters an error. However, when it is successful it will give an str parameter. The contents of the str pointer will remain as it is in the case of an EOF or if it encounters zero character contents (i.e. empty file). In such cases a null pointer is also returned.

The following code is an example of how the fgets function is used:

```
#include <stdio.h>

int main()
{
  FILE * tstfile;
  char tststring [100];

  tstfile = fopen ("thisfile.txt" , "r");
  if (tstfile == NULL) perror ("Error opening file");
  else {
   if ( fgets (tststring , 100 , tstfile) != NULL )
     puts (tststring);
   fclose (tstfile);
  }
  return 0;
}
```

The fputs Function

The fputs() function has the following syntax:

int fputs(const char *str, FILE *stream)

This function will write a string value to *stream. Note that the null character will not be included in the string that will be written to the file. According to the syntax, this function has two parameters: *stream and *str. The first one that appears on the declaration, *str, is an array, which contains the string that will be written. The second one, *stream, is the pointer that points to the file object where the stored string is to be written.

This function will return a positive value when it is successful. In case of failure or when it encounters an error, it will instead return an EOF. The following is a sample code that shows how fputs is used:

```c
#include <stdio.h>
int main ()

{
  FILE *fp;

  fp = fopen("mysample.txt", "w+");

  fputs("This is the first string.", fp);
  fputs("This is the second string.", fp);

  fclose(fp);

  return(0);
}
```

The feof Function

This library function is used to check for the end of a file. It's only value will be either true or false. If the EOF is reached then this function will return true, if the EOF has not been reached in a file then it returns false.

Here is the syntax and declaration of this function:

int feof(FILE *stream)

Here is a sample code that shows how the feof function is used:

while(1)

```
{

    c = fgetc(fp);
    if( feof(fp) )
    {
      break ;
    }
    printf("%c", c);

}
```

In the example above, the feof function is used as the conditional for the if-statement. It means that the program will continue to print the contents of the integer "c" until the EOF is reached in file "fp."

Chapter 13: Graphics Programming Basics in C

One of the best things about the C programming language is that it can also be used to code graphics. Some programmers have even created games using this language. Although a lot of these things may sound really complicated, they're actually not that hard to learn. In fact even if you have no prior background to graphics and visual arts programming, you can learn how to do that in C.

Of course, if your objective is to learn game programming then learning how to do C graphics programming will become an important precursor. Since this book is designed to help beginners, don't expect to be able to make stunning visual displays on your screen with the information contained in here. We will only go over the very basics. After learning the basics, you can move on to more advanced graphics programming.

Note that when you start doing graphics programming in C, you will still need to use the standard library functions. Other than that, you will also make use of the functions that come with the graphics.h and the conio.h headers/library.

The Functions of the graphics.h Header

The first function that you should learn to use is the initgraph function in C. This is the function that will change the screen mode so that it will be ready to output graphics drawings. Needless to say, this is actually the first step that any code will have to take in C. The graphics mode as well as the graphics driver will be passed to the initgraph function.

A different graphics mode will be used once it is initialized, which includes both VGA mode and VGAHI mode (changes the resolution of the screen to 640 x 480 pixels).

The following is a sample code that initializes the graphics mode using the initgraph function:

```
#include<graphics.h>

#include<conio.h>


int main()
{
    int samk1 = DETECT, samk2;
    initgraph(&samk1, & samk2, "c:\\tc\\bgi");
    getch();
    closegraph();
    return 0;
}
```

In C programming, you will use the graphics.h header or if you're using Windows 7, then you'll be using WinBGIM. Either way, the functions you will be using will be used to display different fonts, draw different shapes, and even change the colors on the screen. Using the different functions available, you can make games, animations, and other graphics programs.

Some functions can be used to create shapes like bars, rectangles, lines, circles, and other geometrical figures. You can change line colors and fill colors as well.

The Line Function

One of the very first things that new programmers learn in graphics programming is making a line appear on the screen. This is one of the most basic things that you will be doing. The way this function works is pretty much the same way you will actually draw a line in real life. It begins to create a line from one point and moves off in a straight direction to the other point – two points make a line.

The syntax of the line function is as follows:

line(int x1, int y1, int x2, int y2);

According to this syntax, all you need is to supply the values for x1, y1, x2, y2. You can use constants or variables in each of those arguments. Note that the syntax also specifies that they should all be integers.

Here's a sample code that shows how the line function is used:

```
#include <graphics.h>
#include <conio.h>
 main()
{
  int samk1 = DETECT, samk2;
  int x1 = 100, y1 = 100;
  int x2 = 100, y2 = 100;
  initgraph(&samk1, & samk2, "c:\\tc\\bgi");
  line(x1, y1, x2, y2);
```

closegraph();

return 0;

}

Note that the code above will flash a line on the screen and then disappear. If you want to make the line to pause on the screen a little longer then add a getch line before the closegraph() function.

The arc Function

Let's move the geometry skills up a notch – well, just a little bit. The arc function, as you might have guessed, draws an arc on the screen. It has the following syntax:

arc(int x, int y, int stangle, int endangle, int radius);

The x and y values in this function denotes the center of the arc. The "stangle" integer specifies the starting angle of the arc while the "endangle" integer specifies the ending angle of the arc. The last parameter, "radius," obviously holds the value of the radius of the arc. You can actually use this function to draw a square. You just have to give the starting angle a value of 0 while the ending angle should have a value of 360 (try to review a little geometry to help with that).

The following is a sample code that shows how the arc function is used:

#include <graphics.h>

#include <conio.h>

main()

```
{
   int samk1 = DETECT, samk2;
   initgraph(&samk1, & samk2, "c:\\tc\\bgi");
   arc(98,98, 45, 125, 75);
   closegraph();
   return 0;
}
```

The closegraph Function in C

So far, you've seen the glosegraph() function several times now. Well, here's a short explanation what it is for. This function simply closes the graphics mode that was initialized by the initgraph() function. This same function also frees up the memory that have been allocated by the graphics system. It also restores the screen mode to the original mode. The syntax is simple since all you have to do is to declare the following:

closegraph();

And that's pretty much it. Remember that you should include a closegraph() at the end of your graphics code. You can check out the previous code above to see how this function is used.

The circle Function in C Language

Since you have already seen how the arc function works, then you ought to know how the circle function works. You can't always use the arc function to create circles in C programming. This library function has the following syntax:

circle(int x, int y, int radius);

The x and y integers in this syntax provides the center of the circle. The last parameter in this function indicates the length of the radius. If you notice, the syntax of this function is kind of reminiscent of the formula for a circle in geometry.

The following is a sample code to draw a circle in C language:

```
#include<graphics.h>
#include<conio.h>

main()
{
    int mydriver = DETECT, mymode;
    initgraph(&mydriver, & mymode, "c:\\tc\\bgi");
    circle(50, 50, 100);
    closegraph();
    return 0;
}
```

The bar Function in C

This function draws a rectangle on the screen. The bar is two dimensional and it is filled. It has the following syntax:

bar(int left, int top, int right, int bottom);

As you can see in the syntax or declaration, this function requires both the bottom right corner and the top left corner of the rectangle. Remember that this rectangle will be filled. The current fill pattern will be used. Note that you can change the default fill pattern and fill color as well. To do that you need to use the setfillstyle() function

```
#include <graphics.h>
#include <conio.h>
main()
{
  int mydriver = DETECT, mymode;
  initgraph(&mydriver, &mymode, "C:\\TC\\BGI");
  bar(50, 50, 120, 120);
  closegraph();
  return 0;
}
```

The setfillstyle Function

As stated earlier, this function changes both the fill pattern as well as the fill color used by other functions. It has the following syntax declaration:

setfillstyle(int pattern, int color);
This function has two parameters. The first one is for the fill pattern while the second one is for the fill color. The following are the different fill styles that you can use:

- USER_FILL
- CLOSE_DOT_FILL

- WIDE_DOT_FILL
- INTERLEAVE_FILL
- XHATCH_FILL
- HATCH_FILL
- LTBKSLASH_FILL
- BKSLASH_FILL
- SLASH_FILL
- LTSLASH_FILL
- LINE_FILL
- SOLID_FILL
- EMPTY_FILL

The following is a sample code that uses the bar function. Note that you can change the values of the parameter for pattern. Experiment on the different fill patterns to see how each one of them behaves.

```
#include <graphics.h>

#include <conio.h>

main()

{

  int mydriver = DETECT, mymode;

  initgraph(&mydriver, &mymode, "c:\\tc\\bgi");

  setfillstyle(XHATCH_FILL, red);

  bar(50, 50, 120, 120);

  closegraph();

  return 0;

}
```

The bar3d Function

The bar3d function has the following syntax:

bar3d(int left, int top, int right, int bottom, int depth, int topflag);

As you can see, its syntax is pretty much the same as the one for the bar function. It has two additional arguments, though. Depth returns an int value that will specify the bar's depth. The last argument, topflag, is used to determine whether a three dimensional top should be placed on the bar or not. Note that this function will make use of the current fill pattern and fill color, which can be adjusted as well.

The following code shows how to use the bar3d function:

```
#include<graphics.h>

#include<conio.h>

main()

{

    int samk1 = DETECT, samk2;

    initgraph(&samk1, & samk2, "c:\\tc\\bgi");

    bar3d(98, 98, 120, 120, 10, 1);

    closegraph();

    return 0;

}
```

The ellipse Function

The ellipse function has the following syntax or declaration:

ellipse(int x, int y, int stangle, int endangle, int xradius, int yradius);
This function is used to draw an ellipse at the coordinates x and y, which is the center of the figure. Just like the arc function, it has a start angle and an end angle. The last two parameters of this function indicate the horizontal and vertical radius of the ellipse that will be drawn.

The following is a sample code that demonstrates the use of the ellipse function:

```
#include<graphics.h>

#include<conio.h>

main()
{
  int samk1 = DETECT, samk2;
  initgraph(&samk1, & samk2, "c:\\tc\\bgi");
  ellipse(45, 45, 0, 360, 75, 35);
  closegraph();
  return 0;
}
```

The fillellipse Function

An alternative to the ellipse function is the fillellipse function. It has a simpler syntax, though the parameters sort of look alike. Try both the ellipse and the fillellipse functions to see how each would display on the screen. The fillellipse function has the following syntax:

fillellipse(int x, int y, int xradius, int yradius);

As usual, the x and y values denote the center of the ellipse and the two remaining parameters denote the radii of the ellipse. Try the following sample code and change the values to see what happens to the object on the screen.

```
#include <graphics.h>

#include <conio.h>

 int main()

{

   int samk1 = DETECT, samk2;

   initgraph(&samk1, & samk2, "c:\\tc\\bgi");


   fillellipse(75, 75, 35, 23);

   getch();

   closegraph();

   return 0;

}
```

The cleardevice Function

The syntax for this library function is as follows:

cleardevice();

This function simply clears your screen of any graphics that are displayed. It also sets the position of the coordinates at (0,0). The screen is also filled with the background color that is currently being used.

The following code will show what happens if you use the cleardevice() function:

```
#include <graphics.h>
#include <conio.h>
main()
{
    int samk1 = DETECT, samk2;
    initgraph(&samk1, & samk1, "c:\\tc\\bgi");
    outtext("To clear screen, press a key");
    getch();
    cleardevice();
    closegraph();
    return 0;
}
```

To make the code more interesting, you can draw any of the objects that we have already covered (circle, ellipse, bar, etc.) and then use the cleardevice function to clear the screen. Make sure to add a getch() line before cleardevice(). Now, even though this function acts a lot like the clrscr() function, you shouldn't use that in graphics mode.

The floodfill Function

There are times when you just need to fill a certain section or figure in the screen. You can do that using the floodfill function. Just make sure that the area you intend to fill is enclosed or else the colors will flood and wreak havoc on the screen. This function also uses the current fill color and fill style, which you can modify using the setfillstyle function. The floodfill function has the following syntax:

floodfill(int x, int y, int border);

The x and y parameters will be used to determine the coordinates on the screen. You can call that as the target area or the starting area that should be filled. The last parameter, border, is used to specify the color of the boundary. The following is a sample code that uses the floodfill() function.

```
#include <graphics.h>
#include <conio.h>
 main()
{
  int samk1 = DETECT, samk2;
  initgraph(&samk1, & samk2, "c:\\tc\\bgi");
   setcolor(RED);
  circle(75,75,100);
  floodfill(75,75,RED);
  getch();
  closegraph();
  return 0;
}
```

In this sample code, a circle will be drawn first. After that, floodfill will fill the circle with the current background color. The boundary of the circle will then be colored red. So, you end up with a circle filled with color with its perimeter colored red. Best practice is to use the same x and y coordinates of the figure you are intending to fill (well, so you won't miss and mess up the fill colors).

The getbkcolor Function in C

This library function fetches the current background color in use. It has the following syntax/declaration:

int getbkcolor();

This function returns an integer for the corresponding background color (e.g. if it returns a value of 2 then the current background color is green).

Note that not all of the graphics functions in C language have been covered here. Only the most basic ones have been discussed. If you have gained some interest in creating graphics using this programming language, then you may look for more extensive sources that have been dedicated to this very subject.

Conclusion

Thank you again for purchasing this book!

I hope this book was able to help you to learn the basics of C programming. The next step is to learn the more complex concepts and projects within C.

Finally, if you enjoyed this book, please take the time to share your thoughts and post a review on Amazon. We do our best to reach out to readers and provide the best value we can. Your positive review will help us achieve that. It'd be greatly appreciated!

Thank you and good luck!

Check Out My Other Books

Below you'll find some of my other popular books that are popular on Amazon and Kindle as well. Simply click on the links below to check them out. Alternatively, you can visit my author page on Amazon to see other work done by me.

Android Programming in a Day

Python Programming in a Day

C Programming Success in a Day

C Programming Professional Made Easy

JavaScript Programming Made Easy

PHP Programming Professional Made Easy

C ++ Programming Success in a Day

Windows 8 Tips for Beginners

HTML Professional Programming Made Easy

If the links do not work, for whatever reason, you can simply search for these titles on the Amazon website to find them.